J
623.746
GRE

5247920W
Green, Michael, 1952-
Close air support
fighters
12/04

Woodstock Public Library
7745 Main Street
Woodstock, GA 30188

Woodstock Public Library
7745 Main Street
Woodstock, GA 30188

SEQUOYAH REGIONAL LIBRARY

3 8749 0052 4792 0

WAR PLANES

Close Air Support Fighters:
The A-10 Thunderbolt IIs
by Michael and Gladys Green

Woodstock Public Library
7745 Main Street
Woodstock, GA 30188

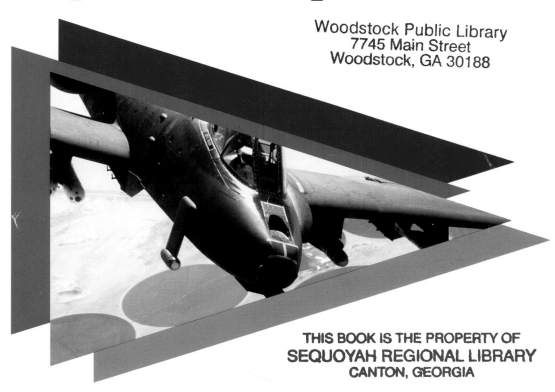

THIS BOOK IS THE PROPERTY OF
SEQUOYAH REGIONAL LIBRARY
CANTON, GEORGIA

CAPSTONE
HIGH-INTEREST
BOOKS

an imprint of Capstone Press
Mankato, Minnesota

Capstone High-Interest Books are published by Capstone Press
151 Good Counsel Drive, P.O. Box 669, Mankato, Minnesota 56002
http://www.capstone-press.com

Copyright © 2004 by Capstone Press. All rights reserved.
No part of this publication may be reproduced in whole or in part, or stored in a
retrieval system, or transmitted in any form or by any means, electronic, mechanical,
photocopying, recording, or otherwise, without written permission of the publisher.
For information regarding permission, write to Capstone Press,
151 Good Counsel Drive, P.O. Box 669, Dept. R, Mankato, Minnesota 56002.
Printed in the United States of America

The Library of Congress Cataloging-in-Publication Data
Green, Michael, 1952–
    Close air support fighters: The A-10 Thunderbolt IIs /by Michael and Gladys Green.
    p. cm—(War planes)
    Summary: Introduces the A-10 Thunderbolt II, its specifications, weapons, missions,
and future in the Air Force.
    Includes bibliographical references and index.
    ISBN 0-7368-2150-3 (hardcover)
    1. A-10 (Jet attack plane)—Juvenile literature. [1. A-10 (Jet attack plane) 2. Attack
planes. 3. Jet planes, Military.] I. Green, Gladys, 1954– II. Title. III. Series.
UG1242.A28G74 2004
623.7'464—dc21   2002156506

Editorial Credits

Christine Peterson, editor; Timothy Halldin, series designer; Patrick Dentinger, book
    designer; Jo Miller, photo researcher; Eric Kudalis, product planning editor

Photo Credits

Defense Visual Information Center (DVIC), cover, 1, 10, 23
Corbis, 20
Photri-Microstock, 4, 24
Ted Carlson/Fotodynamics, 7, 9, 13, 16–17, 18, 26, 29

Consultant

Raymond L. Puffer, Ph.D., Historian, Air Force Flight Test Center, Edwards Air
Force Base, California

1 2 3 4 5 6 08 07 06 05 04 03

Table of Contents

Chapter One

Learn About

- **The A-10's mission**
- **A-10 design**
- **A-10 test flights**

The A-10 in Action

U.S. soldiers are on patrol in a foreign country. It has been a quiet day, but the soldiers know that could change quickly. The ground around them suddenly erupts with large explosions. Enemy ground forces have opened fire.

The U.S. soldiers can hear enemy tanks headed in their direction. The soldiers radio a nearby Air Force base to ask for help. A-10 Thunderbolt II planes arrive in minutes to protect the U.S. soldiers.

The A-10 pilots see enemy tanks in the area. Pilots use large guns that fire shells about the size of soda bottles. Shells from these guns can punch a hole through tank armor. The shells hit the tanks and set them on fire.

Enemy guns open fire to protect the tanks. Many A-10s are hit by enemy shells. The A-10s are protected by heavy armor and keep flying. The A-10 pilots fire missiles at the enemy guns on the ground. The enemy weapons are quickly destroyed. The A-10 pilots fly their planes back to base. Their mission has been a success.

Close Air Support Planes

The A-10 is built to fly missions at low altitudes over combat areas and destroy tanks. This type of mission is called close air support. Planes have been used to attack tanks since World War I (1914–1918). Military officials found that airplanes could destroy tanks better than ground vehicles. Planes were harder for the enemy to attack.

Early kinds of close air support planes were slow and heavy. Gunfire or missiles from enemy troops could easily damage these planes.

The A-10 is called the Warthog due to its odd design.

In 1967, the U.S. Air Force decided to make a better and safer plane for close air support. The Fairchild Republic Company was chosen to build the new plane.

A-10 Design

Engineers designed the A-10 to provide close air support for air and ground forces. The A-10 would fly fast and low over combat areas. The A-10 would be able to make direct hits on enemy tanks. The new plane would strike targets while traveling at a high speed. The plane also would be tough enough to keep flying, even if it was hit by gunfire.

Air Force officials named the new close air support plane the A-10 Thunderbolt II. Pilots nicknamed it the Warthog because of its strange appearance.

Pilots took the A-10 test planes on their first flights in 1972. Production of the planes began in 1975. The A-10s officially entered Air Force service the next year. Fairchild Republic made more than 700 A-10s for the Air Force.

A-10s fly at lower altitudes than other combat planes.

Chapter Two

Learn About

- A-10 cockpit
- A-10 fuel tanks
- A-10 engines

Inside the A-10

The A-10 was designed with certain features for close air support. The plane can take off and land very near to combat areas. The A-10 can use short, rough runways.

Bulletproof glass protects the cockpit from enemy gunfire. Armor protects other parts of the plane. The A-10 can keep flying, even if some parts are shot away during combat.

The A-10 is 53 feet, 4 inches (16.3 meters) long. The plane stretches 57 feet, 6 inches (17.5 meters) between the tips of its two wings.

Cockpit

The single-seat cockpit is made to keep the pilot safe. An armored shell covers the cockpit. A-10 pilots call this armored shell the "bathtub."

The armored shell around the A-10's cockpit is stronger than steel. The protective armored shell can stop gunfire up to 23 millimeters (mm) in size. A 23mm shell is about the same size as a large tube of toothpaste. This kind of gunfire is more powerful than a hand grenade. One 23mm shell is strong enough to blow most airplanes out of the sky. A 23mm shell bounces off the A-10 cockpit's shell without harming the plane.

The A-10 has a head-up display (HUD) in the cockpit. This small screen shows the plane's speed, altitude, weapons, and targets. The HUD is placed in front of the pilot and above the plane's control panel. The pilot can check the A-10's instruments on the HUD without looking down.

An armored shell protects the A-10's cockpit.

Fuel Tanks

The A-10 can carry 10,700 pounds (4,854 kilograms) of fuel. Fuel is carried in four large tanks. Extra fuel is carried in tanks under the A-10's wings. Plastic foam protects the fuel tanks from damage in combat. The tanks will not explode or burn if they are damaged.

Engines

Two General Electric turbofan jet engines power the A-10. One engine is located on each side of the plane. Each engine produces 9,065 pounds (4,112 kilograms) of thrust. Thrust is the force that pushes a jet aircraft through the air. The engines power the A-10 to a top speed of 420 miles (676 kilometers) per hour.

The A-10 flies at a lower altitude than many other combat planes. The plane only flies at an altitude of 15,000 feet (4,572 meters) in combat.

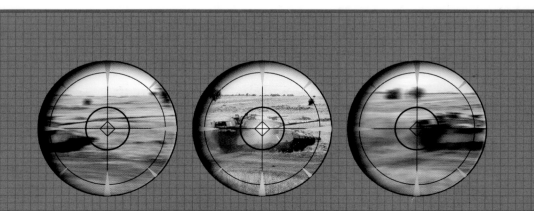

A-10 Specifications

Function:	Close Air Support
Manufacturer:	Fairchild Republic Company
Date Deployed:	March 1976
Length:	53 feet, 4 inches (16.3 meters)
Wingspan:	57 feet, 6 inches (17.5 meters)
Height:	14 feet, 8 inches (4.5 meters)
Engines:	Two General Electric TF-34-GE-100 turbofans
Thrust:	9,065 pounds (4,112 kilograms) per engine
Speed:	420 miles (676) kilometers) per hour
Ceiling:	45,000 feet (13,716 meters)
Range:	800 miles (1,287 kilometers) without in-flight refueling

A-10 Defenses

A-10 pilots have different ways to defend their planes from enemy attack. Pilots fire little bits of metal foil called chaff from pods on the plane's wings. These metal pieces confuse sensors on enemy missiles. The missile explodes in the air without hitting the A-10.

Pilots also use flares to throw heat-seeking missiles off track. Flares stop the enemy missiles from tracking the A-10's engine exhaust.

stabilizer

engine

wing

cockpit

fuel tank

The A-10 Thunderbolt II

stabilizer

engine

wing

AIM-9M missiles

nose

GAU-8 Avenger cannon

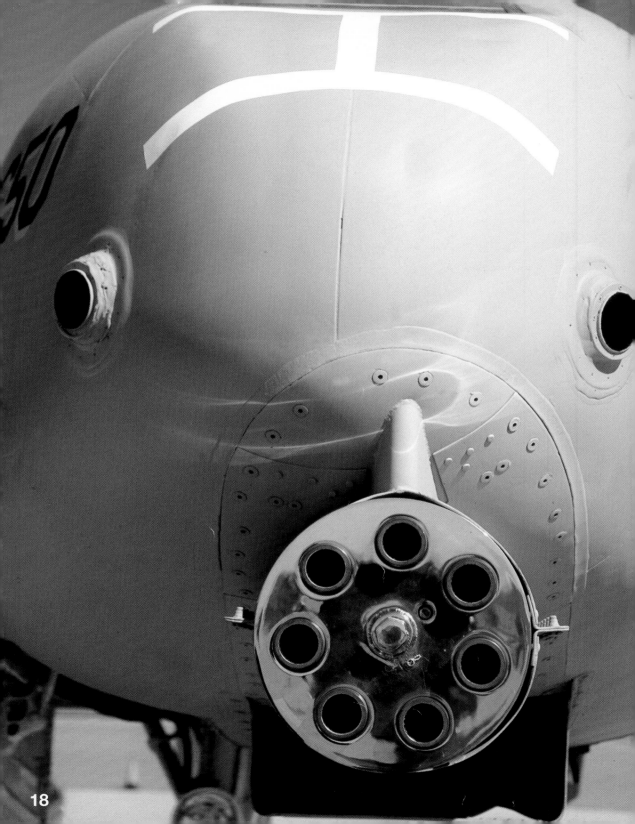

Chapter Three

Learn About

GAU-8 Avenger

AGM-65 Maverick

Air-to-air missiles

Weapons and Tactics

The A-10 has different weapons that can be used in close air support missions. The main weapon on the A-10 is a large machine gun called a cannon. This gun has seven barrels and can shoot several kinds of bullets.

The A-10 carries powerful missiles that are used to attack enemy airplanes and other ground targets. The A-10 also can drop several kinds of bombs.

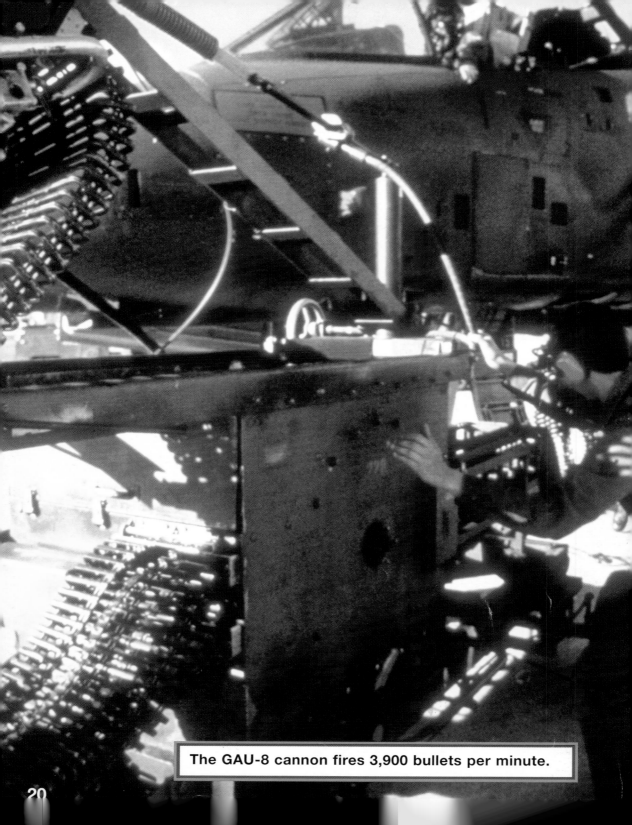

The GAU-8 cannon fires 3,900 bullets per minute.

The GAU-8 Avenger

Close air support planes need guns that can punch holes in tank armor. A-10 pilots use the Gatling GAU-8 Avenger to attack enemy tanks.

The GAU-8 is about the size of a car. This large weapon is almost 20 feet (6 meters) long. An armored shell protects the GAU-8 from enemy gunfire.

The GAU-8 weighs 620 pounds (281 kilograms) without bullets. The cannon holds up to 1,174 bullets. The GAU-8 weighs more than 4,000 pounds (1,814 kilograms) with a full load of bullets.

The GAU-8 can fire 3,900 bullets per minute. A-10 pilots only fire the gun in short bursts. The gun barrels will not get too hot if they are fired in short bursts. Pilots can destroy about 16 tanks with a full load of bullets.

GAU-8 Firepower

The GAU-8 fires two types of bullets. Armor-piercing bullets are used to destroy enemy tanks. The GAU-8 cannon also uses high-explosive bullets to attack enemy trucks or buildings where supplies are stored. Both kinds of bullets catch fire when they hit their targets.

Each bullet fired by the GAU-8 is about the size of a soda bottle. The bullets reach a speed of 3,200 feet (975 meters) per second when fired.

AGM-65 Maverick

The A-10 fires AGM-65 Maverick guided missiles. These missiles are used against ground targets that are up to 7 miles (11 kilometers) away.

The A-10 pilot aims the AGM-65 by looking through a small infrared camera. This camera uses heat to find possible enemy targets. The camera sends a picture to the cockpit. After seeing the picture, the pilot picks a target and fires the missile.

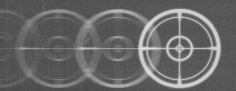

Crew members load an AGM-65 missile on an A-10.

A-10s have been used by the Air Force since 1976.

Other weapons

The A-10 uses the AIM-9M Sidewinder air intercept missile to attack enemy planes. This missile has an infrared sensor in its nose. The AIM-9M uses its sensor to find hot engine exhaust from enemy planes.

LASTE System

Hitting targets with bombs caused problems for early models of the A-10. Pilots were forced to fly A-10s at low altitudes to find targets. A-10s had to get very close to targets before dropping bombs. A-10s were more likely to be hit by enemy weapons at this range.

A Low Altitude Safety and Target Enhancement (LASTE) system fixed the problem. This computer system allows A-10 pilots to locate targets at higher altitudes.

A-10 pilots also drop smart bombs. These bombs use radar or laser sensors to find their targets. A-10 pilots can drop smart bombs when their planes are flying at any altitude. A-10 pilots then have enough time to get their planes out of the enemy's attack range.

Chapter Four

Learn About

- A-10 night missions
- Global Positioning System
- The OA-10

The Future

The Air Force decided to improve the A-10 to keep the plane in service until 2028. This decision was made after the A-10 flew many successful missions during the Gulf War (1991).

More than 140 A-10s were in service during the Gulf War. The A-10s flew more than 8,600 missions and destroyed 960 tanks.

In 2003, A-10s also flew close air support missions as part of Operation Iraqi Freedom.

Night Missions

A-10s are now flying more night missions. Pilots wear night vision goggles (NVG) to help them see better when flying the plane during night missions. The NVG pick up light from the Moon or stars. They turn the light into a picture that the pilot can see.

A better radar system was also added to help pilots on night missions. This radar system finds objects on the ground that pilots may not see in the dark.

Satellite System

A-10 pilots use a Global Positioning System (GPS) to keep track of their planes' locations. This system has 24 satellites that circle Earth. The A-10 picks up signals from the satellites. GPS signals show the plane's exact position.

The GPS also shows where enemy planes and weapons are located. A-10 pilots use this information to quickly fly to targets and avoid enemy weapons.

Night vision goggles help the pilot see better at night.

New Job for the A-10

The A-10 has taken on another job for the U.S. Air Force. Some A-10s were changed to give direct air support for U.S. military ground forces. The Air Force calls these planes the OA-10. The OA-10s carry fewer weapons so they can spend more time in flight.

The A-10 has flown many missions for the Air Force. The plane has the speed and weapons to protect troops on the front lines. The A-10 will remain a strong force in combat for years to come.

Words to Know

bulletproof (BUL-uht-proof)—something that is made to protect people from bullets; bulletproof glass protects the A-10 pilot from gunfire.

chaff (CHAF)—bits of metal released into the air to confuse radar

exhaust (eg-ZAWST)—heated air leaving a jet engine

flare (FLAIR)—a sudden burst of light or flames

infrared (in-fruh-RED)—able to locate objects by heat

pod (POD)—a storage area under the wing or body of an aircraft

radar (RAY-dar)—equipment that uses radio waves to locate and guide objects

satellite (SAT-uh-lite)—a spacecraft that orbits the earth

sensor (SEN-sur)—an instrument that detects physical changes in the environment

To Learn More

Chant, Christopher. *Role of the Fighter and Bomber*. The World's Greatest Aircraft. Philadelphia: Chelsea House, 2000.

Holden, Henry M. *Air Force Aircraft*. Aircraft. Berkeley Heights, N.J.: Enslow, 2001.

Maynard, Christopher. *Aircraft*. The Need for Speed. Minneapolis: Lerner Publications, 1999.

Useful Addresses

Air Combat Command
Public Affairs Office
115 Thompson Street, Suite 104
Langley Air Force Base, VA 23665-1987

Air Force Flight Test Center
History Office
305 East Popson Avenue
Edwards Air Force Base, CA 93524-6595

Internet Sites

Do you want to find out more about A-10 Thunderbolt IIs? Let FactHound, our fact-finding hound dog, do the research for you.

Here's how:
1) Visit *http://www.facthound.com*
2) Type in the **Book ID** number: **0736821503**
3) Click on **FETCH IT**.

FactHound will fetch Internet sites picked by our editors just for you!

Index